RED AIN'T DEAD

150 More Ways To Tell if You're a Redneck

JEFF FOXWORTHY

— ◇ —

Illustrations by David Boyd

LONGSTREET PRESS
Atlanta, Georgia

Published by
LONGSTREET PRESS, INC.
A subsidiary of Cox Newspapers,
A division of Cox Enterprises, Inc.
2140 Newmarket Parkway
Suite 118
Marietta, GA 30067

Printed in the United States of America

10th printing, 1994

Library of Congress Catalog Number 91-061935

ISBN 1-56352-005-2

This book was printed by Data Reproductions Corporation, Rochester Hills, Michigan.
The text was set in ITC Clearface Regular by Typo-Repro Service, Inc., Atlanta, Georgia.
Cover illustration by David Boyd. Cover design by Tonya Beach, Atlanta, Georgia.

Foreword

It is true, as you may have heard, that a comedian's jokes are like his children. You conceive them (not nearly as much fun as with real kids), nurture them, and eventually let them go. Like real children, some are cute, some are bad, and once in a while one exceeds every expectation you ever had for it. That was the case with my "Redneck" jokes.

Appropriately conceived in a cheap motel in Huntsville, Alabama, they quickly grew into more than a comedy bit or even a best-selling book. They became a part of my life. People stop me in airports or on streets and say, "Hey, you're the Redneck guy! And I'm one of 'em!" Excerpts from the first book, YOU MIGHT BE A REDNECK IF..., have been copied, modified, and faxed from workplace to workplace. The material has been "borrowed" by newspapers, wire services, and radio stations nationwide. I feared we had beaten the subject to death, but not a day goes by that someone doesn't offer me a new example of "redneckism." I have received photos of front-yard flower pots made out of old toilets, and newspaper clippings of grooms wearing Harley-Davidson tee-shirts. With the help of my wife and friends, I add several to the list almost daily.

I have collected numerous Redneck lines from radio audiences and even from my live show audiences.

I must admit that I am very proud of my "Redneck child." I am even happier that others love it as I do. So for all those people, here is a second helping. Though conventional wisdom says you can't believe everything you read, in this case I assure you that you can. Red ain't dead.

— Jeff Foxworthy

DEDICATION

To Jennifer, a sister of the finest kind.

ACKNOWLEDGMENTS

Special thanks to all my friends, old and new, who through their laughter and contributions have kept Red alive and kickin'.

You might be a redneck if...

You've been on TV more than once describing what the tornado sounded like.

— ✧ —

You don't need a clean shirt to go to work.

— ✧ —

You think French onion dip is an exotic tobacco product.

You might be a redneck if...

Your local newspaper has a front-page feature called "Cow of the Week."

— ✧ —

Truckers tell your wife to watch her language.

— ✧ —

You've ever stabbed the back of someone's hand while they were reaching for the last piece of chicken.

You might be a redneck if...

When packing for vacation, your biggest decision is whether to use paper or plastic.

You might be a redneck if...

There are four pair of pants and three squirrels hanging from your clothesline.

The family business requires a lookout.

You think the phrase "chicken out" means one of your pets has escaped.

You might be a redneck if...

You slam the door on your truck and your shotgun creates an instant sunroof.

You might be a redneck if...

You have to curl the sides of your cowboy hat so your wife can ride in the truck, too.

You might be a redneck if...

You've ever been getting gas and another
customer asks you to check his oil.

— ✧ —

You have to take the entire day off work
to get your teeth cleaned.

— ✧ —

Your mother has ever been arrested
for poaching.

You've ever been arrested for relieving yourself in an ice machine.

You might be a redneck if...

Your wife's brass knuckles set off the
airport security alarm.

— ✧ —

Anything outside the Lower 48 is "overseas."

— ✧ —

You consider dating second cousins as
"playing the field."

You might be a redneck if...

You've ever been arrested on an
obscene mud-flap charge.

— ✧ —

You've ever eaten out of a minnow bucket.

— ✧ —

Your welcome mat says,
"You'd better have a search warrant."

You might be a redneck if...

You've ever named a child for a good dog.

— ✧ —

The only work your father ever did was
supervised by a man holding a shotgun.

— ✧ —

You converted your carport into
a beauty shop.

You might be a redneck if...

You think the "six to ten pounds" on the side of the Pampers box means how much the diaper will hold.

You might be a redneck if...

You've ever hollered, "You kids quit playing on that sheet metal!"

— ✧ —

You've ever rolled your riding lawn mower.

— ✧ —

Your idea of a summer vacation is running through the sprinkler in the front yard.

You might be a redneck if...

Stealing road signs is a family outing.

You might be a redneck if...

The cockroaches left you a note saying, "Clean this place up!"

You forego a haircut because there's not a clean bowl in the house.

You hold a frog and it worries about getting warts.

You might be a redneck if...

You paint your car with house paint.

You might be a redneck if...

You can eat a McDonald's cheeseburger in one bite.

You might be a redneck if...

You're still upset about "Gunsmoke"
being cancelled.

— ✧ —

You drove to elementary school.

— ✧ —

You have to honk your horn when pulling
into your driveway to keep from killing
chickens.

19

You might be a redneck if...

You've ever lost your wife in a poker game.

You might be a redneck if...

You think safe sex is when the participants
are married to each other.

Your sister subscribes to
"Soldier of Fortune" magazine.

Anyone in your family wrestles
alligators for a living.

You might be a redneck if...

Your wife has four-wheel drive on her
vacuum cleaner.

— ✧ —

The original color of your carpet is an
unsolved mystery.

— ✧ —

You've ever committed a crime with a lawn
mower.

You might be a redneck if...

You think the Nutcracker is something you did off the high dive.

You might be a redneck if...

You say "I heard dat!" more than three times
in a two-minute conversation.

— ✧ —

You know how to milk a goat.

— ✧ —

Everything you won at the fair is hanging
from your rearview mirror.

You might be a redneck if...

You have a tire swing in your house.

You might be a redneck if...

Your local funeral home has a neon sign
in the window.

— ◇ —

You write off a radiator as a business expense.

— ◇ —

Your best pick-up line for women is written
on your baseball cap.

You might be a redneck if...

Your mailbox is made out of old auto parts.

You might be a redneck if...

You've ever vacationed in a rest area.

You might be a redneck if...

You think the Yellow Pages have something to
do with training a puppy.

— ◇ —

You refer to your van as "The Love Machine."

— ◇ —

You have Mason jars filled with stuff
the FBI can't identify.

You might be a redneck if...

Your kids have a three-day-old Kool-Aid mustache.

You might be a redneck if...

You've ever taken out a restraining order
against your mother-in-law.

— ✧ —

You sell rabbits out of your car.

— ✧ —

You think people who have
electricity are uppity.

You might be a redneck if...

Your talent in the local beauty pageant was
making noises with your armpit.

You might be a redneck if...

You have a bumper sticker on your bowling ball.

You might be a redneck if...

Your new sofa was on a curb in another part of town yesterday.

Your two-year-old has more teeth than you do.

Your idea of water conservation is moving your Saturday night bath to every other Saturday night.

You might be a redneck if...

You bring a bar of soap to a public pool.

You might be a redneck if...

All of your relatives' cars have "Tag Stolen"
signs in the rear window.

— ✧ —

You wash your car more often than your kids.

— ✧ —

You're not allowed to mention the game
warden's name in the house.

You might be a redneck if...

You see a sign that says
"Just say no to crack"
and it reminds you
to pull up your jeans.

You might be a redneck if...

Your wife would rather fish off a bridge than shop for clothes.

Your yard has ever been the proposed site for a landfill.

There are tobacco stains down the sides of your school bus.

You might be a redneck if...

Blowing a tire means a new flower pot for the front yard.

You might be a redneck if...

Everyone in your family is an
Elvis impersonator.

You might be a redneck if...

You offer to give somebody the shirt off your back and they don't want it.

— ✧ —

You can give the date and place of every bullet hole in your car.

— ✧ —

Your wife has a set of earrings that you use as a fishing lure.

You might be a redneck if...

Your belt buckle is bigger than your head.

You might be a redneck if...

The Orkin man tells you,
"Give up; you've lost."

— ✧ —

You keep a pellet gun by the front door.

— ✧ —

Your car breaks down on the side of the road
and you never go back to get it.

You might be a redneck if...

You've ever asked a widow for her phone number at the funeral home.

You might be a redneck if...

Any of your hobbies require dogs
and a lantern.

— ✧ —

Your idea of a really big time is shooting rats
at the dump.

— ✧ —

You've ever been the first person in or the last
person out of a video arcade.

You might be a redneck if...

There are antlers nailed to the outside
of your house.

— ✧ —

You've ever left Santa Claus a PBR
and a Slim Jim.

— ✧ —

Your parrot can say,
"Open up, it's the police!"

You might be a redneck if...

You think paprika is a third-world country.

You might be a redneck if...

You wore curlers to your wedding so you would look nice at the reception.

— ✧ —

Your neighbors have ever asked to borrow the light bulb.

— ✧ —

You think "recycling" means going home from work.

You might be a redneck if...

You think toilet water is exactly that.

You might be a redneck if...

You think cow tipping should be
an Olympic sport.

— ✧ —

You shop for groceries at a gas station.

— ✧ —

Your car stereo costs more than your car.

You wet the bed and four other people
immediately know it.

You might be a redneck if...

You come back from the dump with more
than you took.

— ✧ —

Your dog doubles as your dishwasher.

— ✧ —

You live so far out in the country that your
newspaper is yellow by the time you get it.

You might be a redneck if...

Your driveway is bordered by half-buried
tractor tires.

You might be a redneck if...

Your dog can smoke a cigarette.

You might be a redneck if...

You've ever heckled during a eulogy.

— ✧ —

The Roto-Rooter man comes to your house and asks, "What's that smell?"

— ✧ —

Your wading boots double as dress pants.

You might be a redneck if...

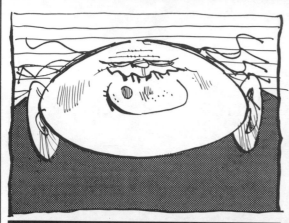

STIFFSOCK COUNTY SHERIFF DEPT.
OA 649-442-9884
JULY 3, 1989

STIFFSOCK COUNTY SHERIFF DEPT.
OA 649-442-9884
JULY 3, 1989

The last photos of your mama were taken
from the front and the side.

You might be a redneck if...

The trunk of your car is tied down and you're
not hauling anything.

— ◇ —

People hunt in your front yard.

— ◇ —

Taking your wife on a cruise means circling
the Dairy Queen.

You might be a redneck if...

Your flashlight holds more than four batteries.

You might be a redneck if...

There is a puddle in your driveway year-round.

— ✧ —

You hang pickled eggs and pop-tops from your Christmas tree.

— ✧ —

Today's dinner was too slow crossing the highway yesterday.

You might be a redneck if...

Your checks feature pictures of dogs fighting.

You might be a redneck if...

Your truck can pass over a 55-gallon drum without touching it.

— ✧ —

Your Christmas tree has a deer stand in it.

— ✧ —

You refer to the fifth grade as "my senior year."

You might be a redneck if...

Your mother gives you tips on how to sneak liquor into sports events.

— ✧ —

Your idea of going formal is a black truck.

— ✧ —

You have a tattoo that says,
"Born to bag groceries."

You might be a redneck if...

All the art in your living room was purchased at gas stations.

You might be a redneck if...

Your wife owns a camouflage nightie.

— ✧ —

Breakfast every morning is interrupted by someone asking, "Anybody seen my teeth?"

— ✧ —

Your muffler is held on by a coat hanger.

You might be a redneck if...

Going to the bathroom in the middle of the
night requires shoes and a flashlight.

You might be a redneck if...

You wake up with Red Man in your hair.

— ✧ —

You keep catfish in your aquarium.

— ✧ —

Your dog rides in the front seat and your kids ride in the back.

You might be a redneck if...

When you talk about great mullet fishermen,
Granny's name always comes up.

You might be a redneck if...

You have orange road cones in your living room.

— ◇ —

You can take your bra off while driving.

— ◇ —

You get Odor-Eaters as a Christmas present.

You might be a redneck if...

Your mother doesn't put on shoes to go grocery shopping.

69

You might be a redneck if...

You walk *into* a restaurant with a toothpick
in your mouth.

You can burp the entire chorus
of "Jingle Bells."

You can't schedule a family reunion until
after the parole board meets.

You might be a redneck if...

You have more than 10 ceramic statues
in your front yard.

You might be a redneck if...

You get your oil changed by your barber.

— ✦ —

Girls' night out is held at the laundromat.

— ✦ —

On your honeymoon you leave
the driving to Greyhound.

You might be a redneck if...

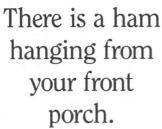

There is a ham hanging from your front porch.

You might be a redneck if...

You can smoke a cigarette to the end without knocking off the ash.

You might be a redneck if...

Your car wakes people up when you drive down the street.

— ✧ —

You have to mow your driveway.

— ✧ —

You give away more free puppies than the Humane Society.

You might be a redneck if...

You can't visit relatives without getting mud on your tires.